PIZZA
ALL AROUND

by dorothy r. colgan

illustrations by vickey bolling

D1405261

The recipes in this book are made with all cooking "levels" in mind.

Quick and easy recipes are indicated by

Medium-difficult recipes are indicated by

Time consuming and/or difficult recipes are indicated by

(P) for PARENT means ALWAYS have a parent or other grown-up help or supervise this step.

Americans love pizza. And most of us think Americans perfected the art of making pizza. But Americans didn't invent pizza! It was actually the Italians who combined foods from Greece and India to create their version of today's basic pizza. Pizza Margherita was the first pizza as we know it to come out of Italy. It was made especially for the queen of Italy in the late 1800s. She loved it so much, it soon became the passion of her subjects and, in no time, the "unofficial" official food of Italy! Now every country has its own favorite version of the pizza — and people can't get enough of it.

Some like it with tuna. Some like it with turnips. Some eat it bubbling hot. Some love it day-old. Some stuff it. Some roll it. Some fold it over.

All around the world, right this very minute, people are gobbling pizza! Whatever the variations, everyone agrees: pizza — that wonderful dough with the endless combination of toppings — is one of the great foods of all time!

Pizza All Around is filled with delicious recipes for all kinds of pizzas, from traditional cheese to unique dessert pizzas. There are step-by-step instructions for pizza from scratch — or if you're in a hurry, there are recipes for pizzas that can be made in a flash!

SAFETY FIRST

Before You Start!

Read through the recipe and be sure you have all the utensils and ingredients you'll need. *Ask a grown-up for permission to use knives, graters, and the oven. Ask for help in setting the oven temperature.*

And Remember These Safety Tips!

- Use only DRY pot holders or oven mitts. (If your mitts get wet, do not use them. Wet ones won't protect you from the heat.)
- Be sure to turn all pot handles away from the edge of the stove.
- When using a cheese grater (which some of the recipes call for if you cannot find packaged grated cheese in the supermarket), keep fingers away from the grating surface.
- When using knives, cut AWAY from your hand. Always use a cutting board.
- Have cooling racks ready for your hot pizza pans.

Kitchen Counting

- **3 teaspoons = 1 tablespoon**
- **4 tablespoons = ¼ cup**
- **5 tablespoons PLUS 1 teaspoon = ⅓ cup**
- **8 tablespoons = ½ cup**
- **16 tablespoons = 1 cup**
- **1 cup = 8 ounces = ½ pound**
- **2 cups = 1 pint**

Note: A standard measuring cup has measurements in cups on one side and ounces on the other. Always use a 1-cup measuring cup to measure flour.

YOUR BASIC PIZZA CRUST RECIPE

Read This First

To make a good pizza, you've got to start with a good crust. You can use this crust recipe for most of the pizzas in this book. It's easy if you follow the directions. And it doesn't take long to make the dough. But before you can begin cooking your crust, the dough must be left to rise for 1½ hours. So if you want to make pizza for dinner, start 2½ to 3 hours before you want to eat.

This Basic Pizza Crust Recipe gives you enough dough for two 12-inch pizzas. Each 12-inch pie will serve 2 to 3 kids, about 2 slices each. Most of the recipes in this book make two pizzas. But there are some that make only a single pizza. Read each recipe carefully and determine how many crusts you will need. If you need only one crust, make the dough rise. Make the whole recipe, then freeze half the do not divide this recipe in half. There would not be enough yeast to dough for another use. (Instructions for freezing and thawing the dough are at the end of the recipe.)

To Begin

Ingredients You Need:

- 1½ cups hot water from your kitchen faucet
- 1½ teaspoons light brown sugar
- 2 packages dry yeast
- 4½ cups unbleached flour
- 1 teaspoon salt
- a handful of cornmeal
- 4 tablespoons (¼ cup) olive oil

Mix the yeast:

1. Pour ½ cup of the hot water into one of your measuring cups. Stir in the brown sugar.
2. Dissolve the yeast in the sugar water, and set aside for 5 minutes. The yeast should become bubbly during this time.

–4–

Mix the other ingredients:

3. Measure 4 cups of flour into a large bowl. Add the salt and mix thoroughly.

4. Make a "hole" in the middle of the flour, and add the olive oil, the rest of the hot water (1 cup), and the yeast mixture.

5. Stir the mixture with a spatula or wooden spoon until it takes the shape of a rough ball. Next put a little flour on your hands. (This helps keep the dough from sticking to your hands and fingers.) Then use your hands to bring the dough together in a tight ball.

6. Put the dough on a lightly floured board or work surface. Knead the dough for 8 to 10 minutes. Push and pound away with the heel of your hand. Keep turning the dough until it doesn't feel sticky. (If it does feel sticky, add a small amount of flour.) Soon the dough should form a smooth ball.

This is Fun!

Utensils You Need:

- measuring cups
- measuring spoons
- large mixing bowl
- kneading surface
- spatula or wooden spoon
- clean bowl for kneaded dough
- rolling pin
- pastry brush
- baking pans:

You can use 12-inch round pans, or rectangular pans or cookie sheets approximately the same size. If your pans have a rim, it will be easier to roll up the sides of the dough. For easier cleanup, it's always a good idea to use non-stick pans. You can also use disposable aluminum pie pans available in most supermarkets. They come in a variety of sizes.

Let the dough rise:

7. Rub a clean bowl with olive oil and place the kneaded dough in it. Lightly moisten the top of the dough with about a teaspoon of olive oil, too.

8. Put a clean cloth or a piece of foil or plastic wrap over the bowl and put it in a warm, dark place, like a closet or cabinet.

9. Let the dough rise for 1 to 1½ hours. It will double in bulk. (That means it will be twice as big as it was when you started.)

10. Punch the dough down with your fist while it's still in the bowl. Then remove it and place on your floured work surface. Knead for one minute more. It should be smooth and satiny.

Roll out the dough:

- For two 12-inch pizzas:

11. Divide dough into two equal parts. Before rolling each one out, flatten the dough ball by pressing it down with your fingers.

12. Lightly dust your rolling pin with flour. Then use it to roll out the dough in a circle shape about 1 inch larger than your circular pan. (If you're not using a circular pan, the dough should be rolled out to a circle approximately 13 inches in diameter.) Be sure to dust the rolling

pin with flour from time to time so it doesn't get sticky. Turn the dough over often while rolling.

13. Have your pans ready, lightly oiled and sprinkled with cornmeal. Transfer each circle of dough to a pan, and with your fingers roll the sides of the dough up ½ inch to make a rim.

14. Brush the dough with a little olive oil. Now comes the fun part — the toppings! Follow any of the pizza recipes in this book or add the toppings of your choice.

Freeze the Extra Pizza Dough

If you're only making one pie, you can store the leftover dough in the freezer for 7 to 10 days. Once you've let the dough rise, punch it down and shape into approximately a 2-inch-thick round loaf. Pack in freezer paper and store. To thaw, place dough in a 250°F oven for 10 to 15 minutes, then remove from the oven, roll out, add toppings, and bake.

You can also use this recipe to make SICILIAN PIZZA CRUST. This is a thicker version of your basic crust and is usually made in a rectangular pan.

DAYS left to my Pizza Party!

SICILIAN PIZZA CRUST

What You Need:

- All the same ingredients used for the Basic Pizza Crust recipe

- **Utensils:** 14-inch rectangular pan instead of a 12-inch pan. All the remaining utensils for the Basic Pizza Crust recipe.

What you do:

- Preheat your oven to 350°F.
1. Follow the Basic Pizza Crust recipe through step #9 in "Let the Dough Rise."
2. After letting your dough rise for 1 hour, punch it down with your fist, cover, and let it stand in a warm, dark area for a second hour.
3. Then, roll out the dough and fit it into your lightly oiled 14-inch pan. Make a rim around the edge by rolling up the dough with your fingers. Let the dough sit in the pan for another 15 minutes. (It should rise just a bit more.)
4. (P) Place the pan in the oven for 10 minutes *without the filling*.
5. (P) Remove the partially baked crust from the oven. Let cool for 5 minutes. Follow any of the pizza recipes in this book or add the toppings of your choice.
6. (P) Return pizza to the oven and complete baking for another 20 minutes or until crust is golden brown and the filling is bubbling.
7. Cool for 5 minutes and serve.

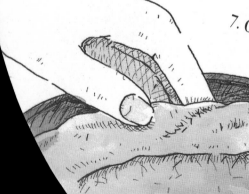

MULTIGRAIN CRUST

Here's a *no-yeast* recipe for a pizza crust with a multigrain twist!

What you do:

• Preheat your oven to 425°F.

1. In a mixing bowl, stir together the first five (the "dry") ingredients on the list.

2. Add the milk and oil to the bowl. Mix well until the flour is absorbed and the mixture forms a sticky ball.

3. Remove the dough ball from the bowl and knead gently 10 to 12 times on a lightly floured work surface. Then press out the dough into your lightly oiled 12-inch pan. (This dough does not use yeast so it does not have to rise.) Fold up the edges to hold the toppings.

4. (P) Place the pan with the dough but no filling in the oven for 12 to 15 minutes or until light brown. Remove from oven and let cool for about 5 minutes.

5. Follow any of the pizza recipes in this book or add sauce, cheese, and toppings of your choice.

6. (P) Return the pizza to the oven and bake for 10 to 15 minutes or until cheese is melted. Let cool for 5 minutes and serve.

What You Need:
for 1 12-inch pizza

• 1 cup oat flour
• ½ cup all-purpose flour
• ½ cup whole wheat flour
• ¼ cup yellow cornmeal
• 1 teaspoon baking powder
• ⅔ cup milk
• ¼ cup vegetable oil

• **Utensils:**
12-inch round pan, measuring cups, measuring spoons, mixing bowls, mixing spoons

-9-

QUICKER CRUSTS FOR PIZZA LOVERS WHO JUST CAN'T WAIT!

If you're in a hurry and don't have time to make the Basic Pizza Crust, or don't have any more pizza dough in the freezer, you can create unique works of art by adding your favorite toppings to these:

- **Frozen Pizza Dough** — Available at most supermarkets; just follow directions on the package.

- **Standard Pie Crust** — If you can't find frozen pizza dough in the supermarket, you can always find frozen ready-made pie crust. This will give you a thin, flaky pizza crust.

- **16-ounce package Hot Roll Mix** — Available at most supermarkets; follow directions on the package for pizza dough.

Y.U.M. TOMATO SAUCE

A good tomato sauce can make a pizza. This one is simple to prepare and tastes amazing! It will make enough sauce for 2 12-inch pizzas.

What you do:

1. (P) Heat the oil in a medium-sized frying pan. Add onion and garlic, and saute (fry in the oil on a low heat) for 2 minutes or until onion is soft. The garlic will be done by that time.

2. Stir in the rest of the ingredients. Cook 15 minutes over medium heat. Do not let the mixture boil.

Tip: If you can't take the time to create your own sauce, you can choose from several prepared pizza sauces at your supermarket. Anything you add fresh to store-bought sauce will make it tastier. Some ideas are fresh chopped green peppers, carrots, celery, zucchini, eggplant, onions, mushrooms, and garlic. (About ¾ of a cup, or a handful of a combination of these ingredients, will add a lot of flavor to your sauce.)

What You Need:

- **4 tablespoons olive o...**
- **5 tablespoons coarsely... chopped onion**
- **1 clove of garlic, minced** (peeled and very finely chopped)

  Note: A head of garlic is made up of a number of smaller pieces called cloves. Use only 1 of these small pieces.

- **2 8-ounce cans tomato puree**
- **1½ teaspoons oregano**
- **½ teaspoon basil**
- **salt and pepper to taste**
- **Utensils:** measuring spoons, knives, frying pan, mixing spoon

TO SAUTE

YOUR BASIC PIZZA
Say "CHEESE"

How you build it:
- Preheat your oven to 400°F.
1. Arrange ½ the mozzarella cheese on the dough.
2. Using your ladle or large spoon, spread the sauce on the pizza to the outside rim. Don't let it all flow to the center!
3. Want to include other toppings? Add them now — in a single even layer across the top of the pizza. See the list on the next page for some suggestions.
4. Sprinkle on the remaining mozzarella cheese.
5. Drizzle (lightly pour drops of) olive oil over all.

How you bake it:
(P) Bake the pizzas — one at a time for best results — in their pans in a 400°F oven for about 25 minutes each or until crust is golden brown. Cool for 5 minutes and serve. *Note: Do not put the pizzas without the pans directly on the oven rack as they do in pizza restaurants.*

TO DRIZZLE

OLIVE OIL

What You Need:
for 2 12-inch pizzas
- **2 Basic Pizza Crusts,** in the pan and ready to bake
- **1 Y.U.M. Tomato Sauce recipe** (or the storebought sauce of your choice)
- **1 tablespoon olive oil** (to drizzle)
- **8-ounce package shredded mozzarella cheese** (or 1 cup of mozzarella that you shred yourself — see instructions p. 13)

- **Utensils:** ladle or large spoon, grater, measuring cups, measuring spoons

To put your own signature on any of the recipes in this book, add your own choice of toppings.

Here Are Some Ideas

There are all kinds of toppings you can use on your pizza, and this is by no means a complete list. Use your imagination. After all, almost anything tastes good on pizza!

- **(P) ground sausage,** fried and drained
- **(P) lean ground beef,** browned and drained
- **sliced hot dogs** (you do not have to precook them)
- **(P) bacon,** fried and drained
- **ham, prosciutto, salami, pastrami, bologna** (cut up or shredded into small pieces)
- **green peppers** (remove stem and seeds and chop into small pieces)
- **anchovies**
- **sardines** (chopped in small pieces)
- **onions** (thinly sliced)
- **mushrooms** (thinly sliced)
- **tomatoes** (sliced or chopped into small pieces)
- **olives** (chopped into small pieces)
- **asparagus** (chopped into small pieces)
- **broccoli**
- **zucchini** (thinly sliced)
- **chick-peas**
- **cooked frozen spinach**
- **precooked pepperoni** (thinly sliced)

To Shred Mozzarella

or Any Other Cheese:

(P) If you are shredding the mozzarella cheese yourself, use a 16-ounce block from the dairy department of the supermarket. Remove packaging, and slide the block of cheese up and down the side of your grater with the largest holes. Keep grating until you have enough for 1 cup. Rewrap what is left of the block of cheese and store in the refrigerator.

PIZZAS WITH E.S.P. — EXTRA-SPECIAL PIZZAZZ!

Mexican Pizza

You don't have to go south of the border to get a taste of Mexico. Create this hot 'n' spicy number right in your own kitchen!

What you do:

- Preheat your oven to 400°F.
1. (P) Heat chili in a medium-sized pot. Add the salsa and simmer uncovered for 10 minutes.
2. Distribute only half the cheddar cheese on the crust and then spread a layer of refried beans on top of the cheese.
3. Next, spoon or ladle your chili and salsa mixture on top of the refried beans.
4. Top with the rest of the cheese and the peppers. Drizzle (lightly — pour small drops of) olive oil over all.

How you bake it:

(P) Bake in a 450°F oven for 20 minutes or until crust is golden brown. For best results, bake one Mexican Pizza at a time. Let it cool for 5 minutes and serve with on-the-side toppings of lettuce, raw onion, and avocado — and a spoonful of sour cream.

What You Need:

for 2 12-inch pizzas

- **2 Basic Pizza Crusts,** in pans and ready to bake (or use a favorite homemade chili recipe)
- **16-ounce can chili** (or use a favorite homemade chili recipe)
- **1½ cups Mexican salsa**
- **1 cup shredded cheddar cheese**
- **15½-ounce can refried beans**
- **¼ cup canned chili peppers** (Careful — these can be very hot to taste! If you don't have a taste for spicy, hot food, you can leave the peppers out.)
- **2 tablespoons olive oil** (to drizzle on top)
- **Optional:** lettuce, onions, 1 avocado (thinly sliced), sour cream
- **Utensils:** medium-sized pot, large spoon or ladle, mixing spoons, measuring cups, measuring spoons, grater

—14—

What You Need:

for 2 12-inch pizzas

- **2 Basic Pizza Crusts,** in pans and ready to bake (homemade or store-bought)
- **3 to 4 cups pizza sauce**
- **1 pound cooked ham,** cut into small chunks
- **½ fresh pineapple,** cut into cubes, or **1 12-ounce can of pineapple chunks,** drained
- **2 green peppers,** chopped (remove stems and seeds first)
- **1 cup grated Parmesan cheese**
- **2 tablespoons olive oil** (to drizzle)
- **Utensils:** measuring cups, measuring spoons, knife, ladle or large spoon, grater

Hawaiian Pizza

Say "Aloha" to a slice from the islands!

What you do:

- Preheat your oven to 450°F.
1. Spoon or ladle the sauce over the pizzas.
2. Distribute ham, pineapple, and green pepper evenly over the pie.
3. Sprinkle on Parmesan cheese. Drizzle (lightly pour drops of) olive oil over all.

How you bake it:

(P) Bake in a 450°F oven for 20 minutes or until crust is golden brown. Cool for 5 minutes and serve. For best results bake each Hawaiian Pizza separately.

THE OFFICIAL PIZZA TIMELINE

Pizza is the most popular food in the USA today. But it was years in the making before it ever hit our shores.

It all started with the crust, then the herbs. *Hundreds* of years later came the cheese. And would you believe that tomato sauce wasn't introduced for hundreds of years after that for one reason only: people thought tomatoes were poisonous! (They belong to a group of fruits well-known to be poisonous. People only used tomatoes for decoration!)

Today the pizza business is a $6 billion industry! Take a look at the official historical pizza timeline and see how the little pie has come so far!

1000 B.C.
Etruscans introduce ashcakes into what is now northern Italy. This is the oldest style of pizza. Romans call it *foccaccia,* which means "fireplace floor bread," because that is where the ashcakes were cooked.

730-130 B.C. The Greeks bring the concept of an "edible dough plate" to what is now southern Italy. They add oil, herbs, olives, vegetables, and cheese. This early pizza becomes a common *breakfast* food during the days of the Roman Empire.

A.D. 600s Herds of water buffalo are imported from India to Italy. The original fresh mozzarella cheese is made from their milk!

A.D. 900s
Parmesan cheese is made in Parma, Italy, for the first time. Its popularity quickly spreads.

Mid-1500s
Spanish conquistadors bring tomatoes from Mexico and Peru, but . . .

1700s ...it takes nearly *200 years* for people to work up the nerve to eat tomatoes, which they think are poisonous.

1905 Gennaro Lombardini opens the first pizzeria in New York City.

1940s U.S. servicemen in Italy during World War II fall in love with pizza. They bring their passion for pizza-eating home with them, and the pizza business booms!

Early 1990s You are here... making pizza history of your own!

Late 1800s Pizza baker Raffaele Esposito, from Naples, Italy, is commissioned to make a pizza for Queen Margherita of Italy. He makes it the colors of the Italian flag: basil leaves for green, cheese for white, and tomatoes for red. She loves it! And even today this basic pizza is called Pizza Margherita.

What You Need:

for 1 12-inch pizza

- **1 Basic Pizza Crust,** in pan and ready to bake
- **8-ounce package of shredded mozzarella cheese** (or a 16-ounce block of mozzarella to grate 1 cup)
- **4 ounces grated provolone cheese**
- **6 ounces ricotta cheese**
- **2 ounces grated Parmesan cheese**
- **2 eggs lightly beaten**
- **2 tablespoons heavy cream**
- **1 tablespoon olive oil** (to drizzle)

- **Utensils:**
measuring cups, measuring spoons, mixing spoons, mixing bowls, grater

WHITE PIZZA

For some people, it's the cheese that really counts. If you're a cheese lover, this is one pie that takes the cake!

What you do:

- Preheat your oven to 450°F.

1. In a bowl combine half the mozzarella with all the other cheeses. Add the lightly beaten eggs and the heavy cream and mix well. Spread this mixture evenly over the dough.

2. Distribute the remaining half of the mozzarella on top. Drizzle (pour small drops of) olive oil over all.

How you bake it:

(P) Bake in a 450°F oven for 20 minutes or until crust is golden brown. Cool for 5 minutes and serve.

NO CHEESE, PLEASE PIZZA

Pizza without cheese — sometimes called *foccaccia*, is very popular. Actually, this kind of pizza bread was around before pizza pies. This recipe is easy and delicious and perfect for friends who don't eat cheese.

What you do:

• Preheat your oven to 400°F.

1. With the palms of your hands, spread dough in a large, lightly oiled rectangular pan, about 24 inches long. Do not roll it with a rolling pin. Let the dough sit in the pan for 20 minutes. This will allow it to rise a little bit more and give it a slightly thicker crust.

2. Spoon or ladle on sauce.

3. Sprinkle a pinch or two of each dried herb on the pie.

How you bake it:

(P) Bake in a 400°F oven for 30 minutes or until crust is golden brown. The temperature is lower and the cooking time is longer than for other pizzas in this book to make the crust chewy on the inside but not burnt on the outside. Remove from oven, let cool for 5 minutes, then serve.

What You Need:

for 1 large rectangular pizza

• **2 Basic Pizza Crusts** (For this recipe do not divide the dough into two halves. Leave in one round ball.)

• ½ to 1 cup **pizza sauce**

• **dried oregano, parsley, rosemary, and basil** (These are basic dried herbs and can be found in any supermarket. Check your own cupboards first. You may already have them.)

• **olive oil** (for pan)

• **Utensils:**
measuring spoons, measuring cups, large spoon or ladle, 24-inch rectangular baking pan

-19-

SEEIN' RED

Sweet Red Pepper Pizza

Here's a pizza pie Peter Piper might have picked. It's made with sweet red peppers instead of tomatoes. This sauce will be tangier than traditional tomato sauce, and the dried pepper flakes will add a hot "kick" to it!

What You Need:

for 2 12-inch pizzas

- **2 Basic Pizza Crusts,** in pans and ready to bake
- **4 sweet red peppers**
- **2 onions**
- ¼ **cup olive oil** (to sauté)
- **1 tablespoon chopped garlic**
- **Optional:** ½ teaspoon dried red pepper flakes (hot to the taste, so be careful!)
- ½ **cup canned chicken broth**
- **8-ounce package shredded mozzarella cheese** (or 1 cup of shredded mozzarella cheese)
- **1 tablespoon olive oil** (to drizzle)
- **Utensils:** knives, medium-sized pot, measuring cups, measuring spoons, mixing spoons, blender, grater, large spoon or ladle

What you do:

- Preheat your oven to 450°F.
1. Cut open red peppers and remove the stems and all the seeds. Slice and chop red peppers into small chunks. Peel the onions, then chop them into small pieces.

CUT RED PEPPER REMOVE STEMS AND SEEDS

CUT INTO SMALL CHUNKS

PEEL, CUT, AND CHOP ONIONS

2. (P) Heat the ¼ cup olive oil in a medium-sized pot. Add the peppers and saute (fry in oil on low heat) for about 5 minutes or until soft. Add the onions, garlic, and dried red pepper flakes. Let the mixture cook for another 5 minutes.

3. (P) Add the chicken broth and cover the pot. Cook for 15 minutes over medium heat.

4. (P) Remove the pot from the stove. Put the entire contents of the pot in a blender or food processor and puree (blend until thick and soupy).

5. (P) Return sauce to the pot and heat until boiling. Reduce heat and cook for 2 more minutes.

6. Arrange half the cheese on the crust and then spread the sauce over it to the outside rim.

7. Sprinkle on the remaining cheese and drizzle (lightly pour small drops of) olive oil over all.

How you bake it:

(P) Bake the pizzas in a 400°F oven for about 25 minutes or until golden brown. For best results, bake each Sweet Red Pepper Pizza separately. Cool for 5 minutes and serve.

OVERSTUFFED PIZZA

Here's a pizza with 2 crusts and the works inside!

What you do:

* Preheat your oven to 450° F.
1. Roll out both dough balls to approximately 12 inches. Put one in the lightly oiled pan, leaving a rim of 1 inch all around.
2. Distribute ½ the mozzarella over the pizza. Spread the sauce over the pizza. Then layer each topping over the sauce: first the spinach, then the sausage, then the mushrooms and the onions, finishing up with the rest of the mozzarella.
3. (P) Place the second crust on top of the filling. Fold the lower crust rim up over the upper crust, then pinch the crusts together to form a seal. Pierce the top with a sharp knife, making an inch slit in 3 or 4 places, to let steam escape.

How you bake it:

(P) Bake in a 450°F oven for 25 minutes or until crust is golden brown. Remove from oven, cool for 5 minutes, and serve.

Note: Because this pizza has two crusts, it will cook best if placed in the lower third of the oven. The top and bottom crusts will cook at the same rate, and you'll avoid burning the top of your pizza.

What You Need:

for 1 large round, stuffed pizza from 2 12-inch crusts

* **2 Basic Pizza Crusts**
* **18-ounce package shredded mozzarella cheese** (or 1 cup shredded mozzarella)
* **3 to 4 cups tomato sauce** (homemade or store-bought)
* **(P) 1 package frozen leaf spinach,** cooked
* **(P) ½ pound sausage,** fried and drained
* **½ cup chopped green peppers** (remove the stem and seeds first)
* **½ cup chopped red peppers** (remove the stem and seeds first)
* **½ pound pepperoni**
* **(P) 1 cup sliced mushrooms,** sauteed
* **1 cup sliced onions**
* **olive oil** (for pan)

Utensils: measuring cups, measuring spoons, knife, grater, rolling pin, large spoon or ladle, 12-inch baking pan

P.D.Q. — PIZZAS DOUBLE QUICK!!!

Want that great pizza taste, without the pizza work or wait? Here are some quick and easy pizza ideas for kids on the run!

Pronto Pizza

This pizza has handy pull-apart sections to make serving a snap!

What you do:

• Preheat your oven to 450°F.

1. Pull biscuits apart. With the palms of your hands, flatten each biscuit into a 4-inch oval. Arrange biscuits on a greased cookie sheet in two adjoining rows. (To grease the cookie sheet, spread one pat of butter all around until the sheet is lightly covered.) Press ends of biscuits together securely. (You are joining the biscuit ends together to make one big crust, instead of individual flattened biscuits.)

2. Combine tomato sauce, onion, garlic salt, and oregano in a bowl. Spread over biscuits to within ½ inch of edges. Top with mozzarella. (In this recipe, you sprinkle all the cheese at once.) Add optional ingredients.

How you bake it:

(P) Bake at 450°F for 8 to 10 minutes or until crust is golden brown. Cool for 5 minutes and serve.

What You Need:

for 2 pizzas, 4 or 5 servings each

• **2 8-ounce packages refrigerated biscuits** (found in the refrigerated or dairy section of your supermarket)

• **½ to 1 cup tomato sauce** (homemade or store-bought)

• **1 teaspoon minced onion**

• **¼ teaspoon garlic salt**

• **¼ teaspoon oregano**

• **3 ounces mozzarella cheese,** shredded

• **butter** (for pan)

• **Optional:** toppings of your choice

• **Utensils:** measuring cups, measuring spoons, knife, cookie sheet, grater, bowl, large spoon or ladle

---

What You Need:
to make 8 mini pizzas

- **8 halves of pita bread, or English muffins, or bagels, or thin slices of French bread**
- **2 tablespoons olive oil**
- **1 cup shredded mozzarella cheese**
- **½ cup grated Parmesan cheese**
- **2 teaspoons dried oregano**
- **Utensils:** cookie sheet, measuring cups, measuring spoons, grater, large spoon or ladle

The Perfect Quick Pita-Muffin-Bagel-French Bread Pizza

What you do:

- Preheat your oven to 450°F.

1. Place each of the bread halves on a cookie sheet, inside half up. Pour a small amount of olive oil over each. (P) Place in oven for 4 minutes (only 2 minutes if using pita bread).

2. (P) Remove from the oven and spoon 1 tablespoon of sauce on each half. Sprinkle ¼ cup mozzarella and ¼ cup grated Parmesan cheese over the sauce. (You can add more or less cheese depending on how you like your Quick Pizzas.)

3. Sprinkle on a pinch of garlic salt and a pinch of oregano. Drizzle (lightly pour drops of) remaining olive oil on top.

4. (P) Return to the oven and continue baking until the cheese is totally melted. 8 to 10 minutes for pita bread, 10 to 12 minutes for all others.

...day with one of these fresh, piping hot pizzas! Note: These ...pes each make one pizza.

Italian Brunch Pizza

What you do:

- Preheat your oven to 500°F.

1. Press dough into lightly oiled pan with palm of your hand. Make outside rim 1½ inches high. Let dough rise in pan for 5 minutes while chopping onions and peppers.

2. (P) Heat the 4 tablespoons of olive oil in a small frying pan. Add the chopped onions and the chopped green peppers and saute (fry in oil on a low heat) for about 5 minutes or until soft. Transfer the ingredients to a bowl and mix in the cheese, salami, and eggs.

3. Season mixture with salt and pepper to taste and pour onto your dough.

4. Drizzle (lightly pour drops of) olive oil over all.

How you bake it:

(P) Bake in a 500°F oven for 15 to 20 minutes or until the crust is golden brown. Let cool for 5 minutes and serve.

- **Utensils:** measuring cups, measuring spoons, frying pan, mixing bowl, 12-inch pan

MOZZARELLA CUBES

What You Need:

for 1 12-inch pizza

- **1 Basic Pizza Crust**
- **1 onion,** chopped
- **2 green peppers,** chopped (remove the stems and seeds first)
- **4 tablespoons olive oil** (to saute)
- **1 tablespoon olive oil** (to drizzle)
- **1 cup mozzarella cheese,** cut into small cubes (To do this, start with the 16-ounce prepackaged block of mozzarella found in the dairy section of your supermarket. Cut enough small cubes to fill a 1-cup measuring cup.)
- **¾ pound salami**
- **6 eggs,** lightly beaten
- **salt and pepper** to taste
- **olive oil** (for pan)

Western Omelet Stuffed Pizza

What you do:

1. Preheat your oven to 450°F.
2. Combine all the ingredients in a bowl.
3. Place the mixture on only one half of your dough shell. DON'T OVERSTUFF!
4. Fold the empty dough side over the filling. Press the edges together to form a seal.
5. Brush the top with olive oil.
6. (P) With a sharp knife, cut a few small slits in the top to allow the steam to escape while cooking.

How you bake it:

(P) Bake in a 450°F oven for 40 minutes or until the crust is golden brown. Let cool for 5 minutes and serve.

What You Need:

for 1 large stuffed pizza
(Do not divide dough into 2 halves.)

- **1 Basic Pizza Crust**
- **1½ tomatoes**, chopped
- **(P) 2 cups mushrooms**, sliced and sauteed
- **1 tablespoon olive oil**
- **½ pound ham**, cut in pieces cubed
- **1 cup mozzarella cheese**, cubed
- **4 eggs**
- **½ teaspoon basil**
- **sprinkling of chopped fresh or dried parsley**
- **olive oil** (for pan)
- **Utensils:** measuring cups, measuring spoons, knife, frying pan, large spoon or ladle, mixing spoon, mixing bowl, pastry brush, 24-inch rectangular pan

Apple and Cheddar Cheese Pizza

For a sweet breakfast treat with a bite of cheddar, try this!

What you do:

- Preheat your oven to 450°F.

1. Roll dough out about ⅛ inch thick. Place in the lightly oiled pan and turn the rim up 1 inch.

2. Spread the apple slices evenly over the dough. Sprinkle ½ cup of sugar and the cinnamon over the apples.

3. To make the topping, put the flour, ½ cup sugar, and butter or margarine in a bowl. Mix together with a wooden spoon until the mixture looks like bread crumbs. Sprinkle this mixture over the apples.

How you bake it:

(P) Bake in a 450°F oven for 10 minutes, then reduce the heat to 350°F for another 25 minutes, or until the apples are tender. (Have your grown-up helper test the apples with a fork to see if they are soft.) Turn off the oven. Very carefully, because the pie is hot, sprinkle the cheddar cheese over the top. Let the pie sit in the turned-off oven for 3 more minutes. Remove, cool for 5 minutes, and serve!

*If you cannot have sugar or don't have a major sweet tooth, this recipe can be made with a smaller amount of sugar or with none at all. Ripe apples will be tasty enough on their own to make this a spectacular treat.

What You Need:

for 1 large pizza

- **1 Basic Pizza Crust**
- **5 large McIntosh cooking apples,** thinly sliced
- **½ cup sugar***
- **1 teaspoon cinnamon**

For Topping:

- **¾ cup flour**
- **½ cup sugar***
- **6½ tablespoons** (about ¾ stick) **margarine or butter,** cut into small pieces
- **1 cup grated cheddar cheese**

- **olive oil** (for pan)
- **Utensils:** rolling pin, knife, measuring cups, measuring spoons, mixing bowl, wooden mixing spoon, grater, 12-inch pan

DESSERT PIZZAS

Tutti Frutti Pizza

A sweeter, dessert-y crust is what makes this pizza special.

What you do:

1. Preheat your oven to 375°F.
   Cover a 10-x15-inch cookie sheet with foil. Slice cookie dough into ⅛-inch-thick slices and arrange them on the sheet, overlapping them slightly.
2. **(P)** Bake at 375°F for 10 to 12 minutes or until the crust is golden brown. Cool, then remove from the foil.
3. In a bowl, combine the cream cheese, sugar, and vanilla. Mix with a wooden spoon until thick and creamy. Spread this mixture over the cookie crust. Arrange the peaches, strawberries, and/or blueberries over the cream cheese.
4. Stir the tablespoon of water into the marmalade, then spoon over the fruit. Chill for about 30 minutes and serve!

What You Need:

for 1 large pizza

- **17-ounce roll of refrigerated sugar slice-and-bake cookie dough**
- **8-ounce package cream cheese, softened** [To soften, take out of your refrigerator about 15 minutes before using.]
- **¼ cup sugar**
- **½ teaspoon vanilla**
- **16-ounce can of peach halves in their own juice**
- **1 pint fresh strawberries** (with the stems and the leaves removed and cut in half), **or 16-ounce package frozen strawberries**
- **16-ounce package frozen blueberries**
- **1 tablespoon room-temperature water**
- **¼ cup orange marmalade**

- **Utensils:** measuring cups, measuring spoons, knife, mixing bowl, mixing spoon, 10" x 15" cookie sheet, aluminum foil

Chocolate Marshmallow Pizza

What you do:

• Preheat your oven to 400°F.

1. (P) Bake your crust without any topping in a 400°F oven for 20 to 25 minutes or until it turns golden brown. Remove from the oven and let cool for 5 to 10 minutes.

2. Sprinkle enough mini-marshmallows on the crust to cover it. Sprinkle the chocolate chips over the marshmallows.

3. (P) Return pizza to the oven for 3 minutes or until the chips are melted and the marshmallows are squishy.

4. (P) Remove from the oven, cool for 5 minutes, and cut into slices. When you pull the slices apart, they will look just like a real pizza, with lots of stringy marshmallows (instead of cheese) and bubbly, melted chips (instead of sauce).

What You Need:

• **1 Basic Pizza Crust,** in 12-inch pan and ready to bake

• **12-ounce bag mini-marshmallows**

• **10½-ounce bag chocolate chips**

THROW YOUR OWN OUTRAGEOUS PIZZA PARTY!

Now that you've tried some of these fun recipes, how about having a full-out pizza party! You and your friends can experiment with recipes you haven't tried, remake your old favorites, and have a mouth-watering time!

There are all types of pizza parties you can have. Here are two ideas to get you started:

PIZZA BUFFET PARTY

If you like variety, the Pizza Buffet Party is the way to go. It's a great way to sample many kinds of pizza and have fun at the same time.

Here's all you have to do:

Send invitations to your best pizza-loving friends. Tell the guests to wear clothes they don't mind getting dirty and to bring their own rolling pins.

A few days ahead of the party, make up enough dough so all your guests will have their own balls of dough. (Remember, each Basic Pizza Crust recipe makes 2 pizzas, so if you're having 6 guests, make 3 batches of dough. Also, remember you can refrigerate the dough overnight or freeze it for 7 to 10 days. See page 7 for a reminder on how to defrost the dough.) You should also prepare a big pot of tomato sauce in advance. You can store this in a covered container in the refrigerator.

You might want to get some disposable aluminum pie pans (approximately 12 inches) as a substitute for baking pans. Buy one for each guest.

Have a grown-up help you prepare the toppings the morning of the party. You'll want to cut up onions, mushrooms, green peppers, pepperoni, sausage, tomatoes, olives, and anything else you like.

Have lots of mozzarella cheese, olive oil, and oregano on hand.

When guests arrive, give them each a work station. They can begin rolling out their own dough and placing it in their pie pans. As soon as everyone is ready, start passing the bowls of toppings around.

Everyone prepares a pizza. Decide on awards to be given for the funniest-looking pizza, the best design, the most toppings, etc.

Have a grown-up be in charge of the baking. (You'll probably be baking more than one pizza at a time, so be sure to allow a bit more time in the oven.)

PIZZA FLIPPING CONTEST

Most professionals agree that pizza flipping is better as a form of entertainment than as a way of making a great pizza crust (which is why it isn't included as a step in making your Basic Pizza Crust). But it's definitely fun, so why not have a pizza flipping contest? Before beginning your contest, make sure you read these tips. Then stand back and watch out. Whoever flips the dough into the most perfect pizza shell wins! (You may want to take a vote on the final outcome or have a designated judge make the final decision.)

1. After letting the dough rise, punch it down, knead for 1 minute, and refrigerate for 15 more minutes. Then shape it into a flat circle about 1½ inches thick.

Wow... what a great trick!!

FLIPPING PIZZA

2. Flour your work surface and start working on the dough at the center. Press it firmly with your fingertips, working from the inside out but avoiding the outer rim.

3. Next, begin stretching it like this: Lift it up and lay the edge over your open fists. Move your hands together and apart, stretching the dough as you go. When you've stretched the dough close to the pan size, but not all the way, you're ready to flip!

4. Center your fists under the dough and raise your fists to shoulder height. Open your hands a little, and begin by bringing your right hand toward you. Quickly change hand positions, flicking your wrists as you bring your left hand closer to your body. Make this one smooth motion. It should send the pizza spinning in the air. Don't fling the pizza up more than a foot until you're really good at this. Practice, practice, practice — and flip away! Don't be discouraged — this is harder than it looks. Soon you'll be able to impress the guys at your local pizza parlor!!!